The Kabbalistic meditations

בס"ד

"Mikdash"
Kabalistic Jewish Meditation "Ways of Peace"
מיקד"ש – מדיטציה יהודית קבלית "דרכי שלום"

Written by: Rabbi Yakov Shepherd
Translated by: Yonatan Pason
Edited by: Josh Bains and Ayalah Shepherd
Type setting and grafics by: Ayalah Shepherd

ISBN: 978-965-7025-69-7

Distributed by:
"Yeshivas Hamekubalim Nefesh HaChaim"
Israeli Non Profit Organization 580628527
For dedications, comments, & classes on
Kabbalistic meditations and much more

Please contact us at:
KingDavidKabbalah.com

Rabbi Avraham Goldstien

Ram Diaspora Yeshiva Toras Yisrael

Moreh Horaha of Mount Zion and Old City

אברהם גולדשטיין

ר״מ ישיבת התפוצות תורת ישראל

ומו״צ הר ציון והעיר העתיקה

בס״ד

I am writing this letter to wholeheartedly recommend "The Kabbalistic Meditations," authored by Rabbi Yakov Shepherd. I have had the privilege of witnessing Rabbi Shepherd's unwavering dedication to helping individuals draw closer to Hashem through kabbalistic meditations and learning.

Throughout the years, I have enthusiastically recommended several of Rabbi Shepherd's publications, and "The Kabbalistic Meditations" stands out as a true gem among his collection. This compilation not only showcases Rabbi Shepherd's profound wisdom and expertise but also serves as a profound tool for anyone who reads and internalizes its teachings. Rabbi Yakov Shepherd's profound insights and loving guidance have the potential to make a profound impact on the lives of those who engage with his teachings.

What sets this book apart is Rabbi Shepherd's unconditional love for mankind. The techniques outlined within its pages have the transformative power to lead individuals towards the pure bliss of drawing closer to Hashem. It is a testament to Rabbi Shepherd's unwavering commitment to guiding others on their spiritual journeys.

It is with great enthusiasm that I extend my humble blessings to all those who embrace "The Kabbalistic Meditations" as a means to deepen their connection with Hashem. May they find tremendous success along their paths and experience abundant happiness within their homes.

May this book bring enlightenment, joy, and fulfillment to all who use it.

With the Blessings of the Torah,

In Loving Memory and Elevation of the Soul of
Rabbi Dr. Yisahar Aaron ben Avraham Avinu,
of Blessed Memory

He dedicated his life to bringing others closer to Torah and mitzvot, teaching both Jews and non-Jews faith and trust in Hashem, with love, reverence, and pure devotion.

He served with dedication and loyalty as a chaplain in the U.S. Army, guiding and inspiring many students on the path of righteousness.

He loved his Creator with all his heart, cleaving to Him in all his deeds, and would always say:
"In all your ways, know Him, and He will straighten your paths."
(Proverbs 3:6)

His love for the Land of Israel burned within him, and he longed to return there, "And the children shall return to their borders." (Jeremiah 31:16)

He bore the yoke of Torah with devotion,
"Yissachar is a strong-boned donkey, lying between the saddlebags." (Genesis 49:14)
"Loving peace and pursuing peace, loving all creatures and bringing them close to Torah." (Pirkei Avot 1:12)

He gave his soul for the sanctification of Hashem's name, fought with all his might for his life, and was known to all as **"a miracle from God,"** until he returned his soul to his Creator.

"Behold, God is my salvation, I shall trust and not fear, for the Lord is my strength and my song, and He has become my salvation." (Isaiah 12:2)

This book, exploring the secrets of Torah, Kabbalah, and meditation, is dedicated to his memory, and to continuing his legacy of bringing hearts closer to the Divine light.

May he soon rise with all the righteous in the resurrection of the dead, and witness the complete redemption and the coming of our righteous Messiah, **"And they shall come to Zion with joy, everlasting happiness upon their heads."** (Isaiah 35:10)

May his soul be bound in the bond of eternal life.

This dedication is written in honor and memory of
Rabbi Dr. Yisahar Aaron ben Avraham Avinu, of blessed memory.

This book is dedicated to the health of body and soul, to long and
healthy lives, and to the protection of his beloved children, and widow
that they may be blessed with light, joy, and prosperity:

ɞ **Zalman Leib ben Tamar**
ɞ **Menachem Mendel ben Tamar**
ɞ **Moshe Chaim ben Tamar**
ɞ **Rivka Jamila bat Tamar**
ɞ **Gavriel Noach Chai ben Tamar**
ɞ **Menucha Rachel bat Tamar**
ɞ **Ittai David ben Tamar**
ɞ **Boris Ben Zion ben Tamar**

May each of them be granted complete health, lives filled with Torah,
wisdom, and abundant blessing, divine protection, success in their
paths, and love and reverence for Hashem in all they do.

"I am Hashem, your Healer." (Exodus 15:26)
"Length of days is in her right hand; in her left, riches and honor."
(Proverbs 3:16)

May this book serve as a merit for them, and as an elevation for the
soul of their dear father, who left behind a legacy of blessing and
eternal wisdom.

May you all be blessed with long and good lives!

Introduction

My Vision of a Perfect World

Right now, I'd like you to imagine a harmonious world, where the profound practice of Kabbalistic meditation is embraced and cherished by all.

As people, like you and me, immerse themselves in the depths of introspection, their character undergoes a profound transformation...

It elevates them to live by higher standards of values and morals, which creates a global community.

And this is how it feels:
You begin each morning with a sense of purpose. With deep awareness, as you find solace by connecting with higher dimensions—through the Ohr Ein Sof within yourself, which is the highest level of your soul.

You enjoy inner peace, clarity, and a profound connection to both yourself, other people, and our Creator. Conflict and division give way to harmony and collaboration as we all perceive that we are interconnected
.

As you tap into your innate creativity, intuition, and resilience—you automatically contribute to society and the world according to your essence.

Schools that use the teachings of Kabbalistic meditation will nurture future hearts and minds, helping children grow up with a deep understanding of their spiritual nature, developing emotional intelligence and a strong bond with God. Children will learn to embody the values of kindness, empathy, and responsibility—creating a compassionate and everlasting world for generations to come.

We share a collective recognition that each person holds a unique spark of divine light.

Everyone is encouraged to shine their light brightly. To embrace their true purpose and gifts. The holy spark within everyone, is dressed with different garments by different people nations and cultures. This makes our lives diverse in one hand and on the other untided.

May this vision inspire us to embrace the practice of Kabbalistic meditation. Let us manifest a world of harmony, love and spiritual fulfillment together.

This book will introduce you to authentic Jewish meditation. It is deep, and based on the practice of Kabbalah. Although these meditations have been practiced exclusively by a select group of Jews over the centuries, the fundamentals of kabbalah can be used to connect with God by anyone with a sincere heart, and a concerted mind.

Using this book, you can develop a keen awareness of your own purpose, and the purpose of all reality.

As the prophet Eliyahu said:

"I call on heaven and earth to witness that any individual, man or woman, Jew or Gentile, freeman or slave, can have Divine Inspiration descend upon him."

Such a level is very difficult to attain. However it's important to realize that it *IS* possible to reach unimaginable spiritual heights.

This is how:
- Zealously learn and guard all the details of the Seven Noachide laws, (or if you are Jewish, the 613 laws of the Torah.)
- Hone your character traits to a razor's edge—such as humility, forgiveness, kindness, patience, faith, greatitude, and trust in God.
- Follow the meditation techniques and advice in this book.

In one sense, it is very simple. However, it takes incredible commitment to self-elevation. Regardless of your current level—this book gives you the internal roadmap to speak to your creator, and refine yourself using mediation. If you are looking for a new way to awaken your spirituality, the practices in this book will give you an incredible way to gain self-understanding, personal satisfaction, elevation and a stronger connection to God.

Chapter 1:
Ascending the Path of Meditation

Meditation 1: Foundation

Authentic meditation begins with mastering the art of mind control. With the techniques in this book, you are going to liberate yourself from the labyrinth of thoughts, and break free from the veil that limits the boundless potential of your mind.

This is the start of most kabbalistic meditations, and we will refer to it in subsequent meditations as the Foundation. (Remember to do this in a safe place, Do not meditate while operating heavy machinery, or driving, or need to be on aleart[ie. watching children]).

Isolate yourself. Switch off your devices and distractions. For the best results, ensure you can have total concentration.

Get comfortable in a chair or on a cushion. Sit with your back erect and your head straight. When the spine is in its natural position, it is easier.

Breathe deeply and hold it for just a moment. Then, let it out slowly. Focus on the sound and feel of your breathing. Close your eyes. Bring your breath to the center of your focus. Imagine you are inhaling and exhaling light. With every breath, relax more. (many

enjoy imagining the breath as it enters the the nose
and does a circle from the back of the body between
the muscles down to the feet then up again and out the
mouth. cleaning and clearing all the negativity form
the body.)

Notice the voices and thoughts in your head. Don't
worry about them. They are inevitable! Simply note
every mental distraction, and let it pass as you bring
your attention back to breathing. Imagine them flying
away. You can even smile. There's no need to be too
serious. Always bring yourself back to the comforting
light of your breath.

After completing the meditation, gradually open your
eyes. Take a moment to express gratitude for the
precious time you've dedicated to yourself, even if it
was just for a brief five minutes.

As you continue learning, aim to extend your practice
gradually. Remember, even after exploring all of the
techniques, you can always revisit and enjoy this
foundational meditation.

Meditation 2: Writing

Reach a state of mindfulness, and write your thoughts.

Here is a simple, yet powerfully revealing meditation exercise. Get a notepad and a pen, so you are ready to write.

- Repeat the Foundational meditation. (This is all the steps in meditation one –as you grow in skill, this will come easier and faster.)

- Once you've arrived at a clear sense of mind, pick up your pen and begin to write.

- Write all of your thoughts. It might be words, letters or anything that comes to mind. Alternatively, you can say whatever comes to mind out loud.

Journaling, the power to write our inner thoughts, will bring to light a deeper understanding of ourselves. Writing is even used in some therapies as a primal way to listen to your inner voice and reframe ideas, feelings and experiences.

It was practiced by the renowned kabbalist, Rabbi Avraham Abulafia. He would rearrange the letters of words he wrote or spoke, morphing their meanings to open new spiritual pathways.

Hebrew is called *Lashon HaKodesh*, which means *holy language*. In Kabbalistic terms, the Creator used Hebrew letters to form all things, across many dimensions. Speaking Hebrew words gives us a powerfully metaphysical way to ascend levels of kedusha or holiness. Literally, kedusha means separation.

Kabbalistic meditation, properly performed, allows us to separate ourselves from the physical world, and enter the many worlds of the spiritual.

Meditation 3: Awareness of the Body

Relax your body, toes to scalp. Contemplate that the real you is a neshama within your body.

Meditation begins with our bodies. We use the physical world to carry, and care for the *neshama*—our soul. Far from denying our bodies, this mediation will get us in touch with the physical, which is meant to serve as a chariot for the *neshama*.

Begin with the Foundation meditation.

*

Once you are in a meditative state, focus on your body. Begin at the bottom, which is the lowest part of yourself, both physically, and spiritually. Focus only on the toes. Relax them. Then relax your feet.

Mentally, make your way up, giving attention to relax the rest of your body. Focus only on one part at a time. Move up your calves, thighs, waist, abdomen, torso, arms, neck, face and head.

Accomplishing total relaxation of the entire body is a very powerful state. Feel satisfaction when you've done it!

Then, take it further: become aware that *you* are not your body.

Your body is a vessel that holds *you*.
You are your soul.

Know that each part of your body corresponds to a part of your soul, which is unbelievably high in the orders of Creation.

On a very deep level, your soul corresponds to the powers of Creation that God used to make and control everything. These powers are called the *Sefirot*—a major aspect of *kabbalistic* understanding and practice.

Each person is a mirror of all Creation, and of the

sefirot themselves. This awareness brings holy light, a light of *kedusha*, down to your soul and body.
Light, in Hebrew—*ohr*—is another major aspect of *kabbalistic* meditation. While we never imagine what the Creator "looks" like, we do imagine ourselves interacting with the emanations of our Creator, which we experience as formations of light.

So, to finish this mediation, imagine a bright white and pure light that is both covering and filling your body.

Bask in the light. Feel it's warmth, energy and Kedushah.

Meditation 4: Awareness of Emotion

Contemplate on your emotions, becoming aware of them, as you bathe in heavenly, loving light.

Your soul is made of different aspects. The first level of your soul is called the *Nefesh*. This is your animal soul, and is little elevated from the spiritual animating force in all life on earth.

However, human beings are far more than mere animals. We are infinite souls inhabiting earth in bodies of flesh and blood. We are the level above angelic beings. We have emotions, and our emotions are associated with the level of the soul called *ruach*.

Ruach is an intermediate level of the soul, between our animal nefesh, and the *neshama*, which is the highest soul itself (there is also *Chaya* and *Yechida* which are tecnicaly higher). Just as we tend to feel our emotions within our hearts, the *ruach* is found and manipulated within the heart.

Contemplating our emotions will help us to tap into this level of the soul, and it's a very powerful practice when achieved.

Begin with the Foundation meditation.

Once in a meditative state, be aware of what you are feeling emotionally. This is just as much part of your experience as your physical sensations, and your thoughts.

Sometimes you might be depressed without realizing it. Become aware of what you are feeling. Then, whatever it is, accept it, and next—try to reconnect with God by kindling joy and happiness.
Perhaps the quickest way to this emotion is to have *Hakaras haTov*: Notice and acknowledge the good in your life. Feel this good feeling of gratitude to a physicall level, therefore lifting you out of sadness, and restore your positive emotions.

Once you're in control of your emotions, try going higher. With every breath, you can become more open to experiencing spiritual contentment. (Some people might even feel bliss.)

Conjure in your mind the image of a bright light, which in kabbalistic meditation is emitted from the Ain Sof, or from The Creator, that is without end. At the highest level of creation, this light is so far away that it's source is impossible to reach. And yet, we are touched by it's light. Allow this illumination to fill your heart. Let it transform your negative emotions into happiness and joy.

From this emotional state, we are far more receptive.

Kabbalah teaches that navuah: prophecy, or Ruach HaKodesh: divine inspiration can only be received in a state of simcha: joyful happiness. While relatively few people have ever attained these levels of amazing connection, we can all elevate our conscious awareness and depth of meditation.

Don't be afraid to use inspiring music; you will be following in the footsteps of the King David, and the prophets and Levi`im in the ancient Israel.

Both used music to lighten their hearts, and connect to God in uplifting, meditative prayer. Kabbalah teaches that we cannot receive divine inspiration in a sad or angry state. True happiness and love are needed to receive prophecy.

Meditation 5A: Transforming Negative Emotions and Pain to Inner Strength

Meditate on a past experience that caused you pain, as if you're watching a movie. See the good. Find God's hand behind the scenes and forgive the people who hurt you—throwing away the negative emotions.

This Meditation is designed to help deal with negative situations, **which are not traumatic.**[1] It can help you find closure, understanding and inner peace.
If you're dealing with acute trauma, or intense emotional distress, do not do this mediation alone.
Rather, seek the guidance of a trained professional who specializes in trauma therapy.
A qualified expert can be instrumental in your healing.

Begin with the Foundation mediation.

Move back in time to an event that caused you to feel negative emotions.

In your imagination, let the incident unfold as if you are seeing a movie, from a third-person perspective. Be distanced from the screen.

While it might be painful to watch, try to change your

[1] Treating Trama or PTSD is serious, and should be worked on with a trained profesional, these mediations are here to help deal with daily stress and negativity.

perspective on the situation. Change the coloring and make the movie smaller. Can you find something good in what happened? Is there a way you can feel positive emotions about it, and anything you might have gained or learned?

This is only happening within your mind, so if you want, you can change the way the event took place. Imagine the outcome was truly positive. *(every memory is a distortion of the truth, there is not objective memory, but the distortion can have a profound affect on us. Therefore we can make a positive distortion)*

While in the meditative state, consider that God is not only responsible for this incident, but created it for your benefit. The only thing we lack is understanding why.

Search for good things that have arisen in your life directly because of this negative incident. Feel gratitude for them, and recognize they came from something that was painful.

This is a powerful way to heal negative experiences to reframe events that have been holding you back. If you are able to forgive others, and yourself, and truly imagine that things happened differently this meditation practice can have profound healing effects.

However, if it is too painful—skip it!

It might be too traumatic if you are having negative

looping thoughts, which you cannot stop. Phisicaly shake your body and think of something that makes you happy. In this case, it is wise to speak with someone—a friend, spiritual advisor, and ideally, a professional therapist, who can help you process the pain.

Meditation 5B: Earliest Memory

Meditate on your earliest memory.
See it in detail for as long as possible to find new facets, and reframe the experience as an adult—gaining healing and understanding.

This is designed to help you heal emotional wounds from childhood. If what you are dealing with is too painful, seek a professional therapist.

Begin with the Foundation.

Try to remember your first childhood memory. (An early memory is good, too.)

*

Once you have it, you will likely feel emotions. Remain with these feelings. Contemplate them. See every detail and envision the experience more fully than you have before.

*

Consider what happened. As you meditate, review it from your adult point of view.

*

What changes? What can you heal from this memory, with all of the life experience you now have gained from that moment to this one?

While these are not seemingly "spiritual" experiences, they are profound, healing and give you clarity, health and vitality—which are all prerequisites of gaining spiritual insight.

Meditation 6: Object Contemplation

Choose an object to contemplate in mediation. Consider: It is not only created and sustained by God... it reveals God to you, personally.

Having dealt with some memories from the past, we'll now meditate on something in the present.

Begin with the Foundation.

*

Keep your eyes open. (Yes, you can practice meditation with open eyes.)

*

Choose an item to focus on.

*

As you meditate, consider that it was brought into existence by the Creator of all things.

It is also sustained by Him, right now.

Meditate on how God is revealing Himself, using this object—to you personally.

This is an extremely powerful Kabbalistic meditation technique, because it enables you to see the Creator in all things.

In Hebrew, this world is called olam, which means hidden. Mediating on the spiritual reality of an object is like perceiving a curving face behind a veil.

Meditation 7: God Is One

Contemplate that God is One. See the goodness in all things, know that God is the source, and feel gratitude—with this emotion, nullify yourself within God. Surrender your sense of being and feel the bliss of ultimate connection.

At this point, we have reached the primary goal of mediation, which is connecting with God using all parts of creation:
- your body
- mind
- memory and imagination (past, present, future)
- physical objects

...God, however, has no parts. There is nothing exept of God.

God is the source of all things. The good and the bad both lead back to God. For all humans, this is the ultimate dilemma, and the ultimate wellspring of faith. Untold numbers of sages have died under torture and grave injustice while meditating on the words "God is One." When you seek God with sincerity, pure in purpose, you will—at some point—begin to experience moments of what the sages felt: Awe and tranquility, even in difficult circumstances. What today, some psychologists call...grit.

Begin with the Foundation mediation.

Contemplate that ALL things and circumstances are from God.

Contemplate the idea that God is One—there are no parts.

Because we do have parts, this is an abstract idea we can never fully comprehend. Spending time with it will build our spiritual capacity and allow us to transcend our limited points of view.

As you consider this you may naturally feel a need to see that what God does is good.

Notice yourself filling with gratitude.

At this point, nullify yourself within God. Surrender your sense of being and feel the bliss of ultimate connection.

Know that God is the source of all love and all good. Everything is for the sake of unity.

✳

Understand and recognize that you are very much loved.

✳

Let God guide you. Know that you are very much loved.

✳

Return slowly back to yourself and write what you experienced emotionally, physically and mentally.

Be patient.

It will take you a great deal of time and practice to develop the spiritual, mental and emotional strength to perform these techniques in one sitting.

Enter these lofty meditations with loving emotions and you will connect with God at an extremely high level, feeling joy and love, which protect and heal you.

Awareness of the Truth

It's one thing to dabble in meditation. It's another to spend all of your time meditating. It's majestic, and impractical. And yet this is the level of meditation practitioners who have aligned themselves with *shvisi*—placing an awareness of the Creator on their consciousness at all times.

This is possible.

In fact, it is the first of the instructions in the mystical texts of Jewish law, which is inscribed for all of the nation's people, not only the Kohanim, accomplished scholars and Kabbalistic masters.

Awareness is fundamental. Kabbalistic mediation will help us to build our own muscles of awareness.

Mediation 8: Godly Mediation

Contemplate and internalize that God is one, and all He does is good.

Now we will introduce concepts based on the Hebrew alphabet. This is intrinsic to the underpinnings of Kabbalah, because according to Jewish tradition, the world is created from Hebrew letters. Called lashon hakodesh, the holy language.

A Kabbalist would never place a Holy book on the floor, or take it into the bathroom. So too, it is not appropriate or productive to think of Hebrew meditations in the bathroom or any unclean place—it is the letters and words themselves that are vessels of holincss, whether you read, say or think about them.

The following meditation will force you to reconsider your hardships in light of God's goodness. Whether or not, you can fully accomplish this, it will forsure cause a profound transformation in your ability to see the good in all things.

Contemplate that God does all, and all He does is good.

*

Meditate on the knowledge that everything unfolds for your best, and that—in reality—there is no inherent negativity in your life.

*

Imagine the Hebrew letters

אין עוד מלבדו

(Devarim 4:35). These are pronounced *ein od milvado*, and means: There is nothing besides Him. As you picture the words and say them, work on accepting His sovereignty, going under His protective wing.

*

Place your right hand over your eyes and repeat three times:

אין עוד מלבדו

Now you are adding powerful words to your mediation. The words, which you have just said, is acknowledging the fundamental concept that God is One.

*

Begin speaking to God, and say in an undertone: Nothing can happen to me unless You will it, and if You will it, then it is good for me, and my family. No one has the power to hurt me or do me good if You do not permit it. Keep repeating these words.

How does it feel?

Meditate on gratitude and say:
Thank you, God. I am in Your Hands. No one else influences me. Only Your Will determines what is good or bad for me. I wholeheartedly trust in you. Whatever happens to me is for my own good.

If you are in pain or suffering, thank God for the pain, and for the good in it.
Consider the emotions it has brought you, and the opportunity to elevate spiritually. Of course, you can always speak to God as long as you need or wish.

Return slowly from your meditation, and then write what you experienced emotionally, physically and mentally.

This is not an easy meditation. If you are in pain, it can cause you to feel a lot of emotions. When you are able to put your whole being into the big weight off your shoulders. [2]
**A chart is provided for you at the end of this book. Use it to record your insights and growth as you continue mastering kabbalistic meditations.

2　　There is a whole system brought down from the Baal Shem Tov, on how to change reality with Gratitude, and accepting reality as a gift from God.

In this system we Thank God for our troubles, and we thank God for each and every emotion that came because of it. We afirm Gods sovereignty, That God is the cause of everything that happens to us, and that it is all for the good. Only after that do we request positive changes.

Chapter 2:
Meditations of Love

One of the deepest axioms in the Torah is to *"Love your neighbor as yourself."*

But, how can we truly apply this principle to others if we haven't learned to love ourselves first?
The initial step is to understand how to cultivate self-love, which will then enable us to extend that same love to those around us.

If you find yourself unsure about your level of self-love, here is a brief questionnaire that can help you gain clarity.

Circle what best describes yourself

1. Usually I say what I think

1	2	3	4	5
Not at all				Very True

2. I feel stable even when i am stressed

1	2	3	4	5
Not at all				Very True

3. Usually I have the tendency to love and accept people.

1	2	3	4	5
Not at all				Very True

4. Usually I know whats good for me

| 1 | 2 | 3 | 4 | 5 |
| Not at all | | | | Very True |

5. I am successful in what i do

| 1 | 2 | 3 | 4 | 5 |
| Not at all | | | | Very True |

6. Usually its easy for me to forgive and Forget.

| 1 | 2 | 3 | 4 | 5 |
| Not at all | | | | Very True |

7. Most of the time I am happy and joyful.

| 1 | 2 | 3 | 4 | 5 |
| Not at all | | | | Very True |

8. When I look at myself in the mirror i am usually smiling.

| 1 | 2 | 3 | 4 | 5 |
| Not at all | | | | Very True |

9. I am quite happy with the way I look

| 1 | 2 | 3 | 4 | 5 |
| Not at all | | | | Very True |

10. Most of the time I am energetic

| 1 | 2 | 3 | 4 | 5 |
| Not at all | | | | Very True |

11. Usually i can control myself.

| 1 | 2 | 3 | 4 | 5 |
| Not at all | | | | Very True |

12. Usually I am achieving my goals.

1	2	3	4	5
Not at all				Very True

Please add up all the numbers you circled,

If you scored between 45-60 you love andvalue yourself above average you have a good sense of self confidence and you think about yourself in a positive manner.

If you scored between 30-44 usually you love and appreciate yourself above average most of the time you are self confident and usually you think about yourself in a positive way.

If you scored 15-29 like most of the people in the world you like yourself you have the tendency to criticize yourself but yet there are some parts of life that you are Confidant. You think and feel about your self in a mixed way, bouncing back and forth. The meditation you will find in this book will help you gain more positive feelings

If you scored 0-14 congratulations you are about to have a life changing opportunity if used correctly. Until today you have had a strong tendency to criticize yourself and put yourself Down. By practicing the following meditation regularly you will be able to open a new page of your relationship with yourself, God, and that will expand to all the people around you. Who will Ascend the Mountain of God?

By practicing the following meditation regularly, you will be able to forge a new relationship with yourself and others, and that will expand to all the people around you.

Meditation 9: Self Love Meditation

In meditation, merge with someone who you love or admire. Absorb the love that you generate and try to feel how it increases and strengthens the positive qualities you have inside.

Remember, the initial stage of authentic Kabbalistic meditation involves freeing yourself from all thoughts and releasing the hold of illusions that restrict your mind's freedom.

Begin with the Foundation meditation.

Think of someone who can be a role-model for you. He or she can be a source of inspiration, love and acceptance.

It doesn't need to be someone you know, or who knows you. It can be someone from the past—even if you knew only briefly.

Continue to breathe, and think about this person. What aspect of character allowed him or her to give you love and support?

✳

Envision yourself merging with this person, and immerse yourself in their perspective. Visualize yourself experiencing life through their eyes, as if you were the same person. Allow yourself ample time to connect with the emotions and characteristics of this person.

✳

Now, shift your perspective. See yourself through their eyes. Tap into the love they feel for you.

Notice the emotions and sensations that arise, and try to articulate how your mentor perceives you. What do they see in you that ignites such profound love? What are the qualities that make you worthy of their love and affection?

✳

Absorb the love that you generated with this meditation and try to feel how it increases and strengthens your own positive qualities.

✳

Now, move the feelings from your friend, to God. Elevate your consciousness to a higher level, and try to feel how God is watching over you, and loves you. Imagine a big white light coming from God that radiates love, peace, happiness and patience. Absorb these qualities. Put your two hands over you heart, right over left. Breathe deeply and enjoy the experience.

✳

Say aloud the following, or your own version of it:

I am a human being created in the image of God. It is possible for me to love and to be loved. I thank you God, for creating me the way I am. For giving me so many positive qualities.

(let yourself ponder on them)

Please help me to learn to love and cherish all the goodness that you give to me, and the people around me. Guide me in cultivating and enhancing these positive qualities within myself.

What changes when you do this meditation?
What are the positive outcomes?

The more that you repeat this meditation, the more you increase the infinite light and love within yourself, which will minimize and weaken negativity.

By increasing light, darkness disappears. Write in your journal what you experienced emotionally, physically, and mentally.

Meditation 10: Interpersonal Love Meditation

Connect with the love others have for you. Extend that love to people who you find difficult. By visualizing God's all-encompassing love, and projecting this divine light to others, you foster a deeper connection with both them and God, enhancing positivity and reducing negativity without struggle.

Love is the catalyst for spiritual advancement. Once you start giving love to yourself, you can begin offering it to other people. Even people who you have a hard time with.

Start from steps 5 and 6 in the previous mediation: See yourself through your friend's eyes. Tap into the love he or she feels for you. Feel how it increases and strengthens your own positive qualities.

＊

Now, you are ready to do something harder; imagine a person who you are having a difficult time loving, or accepting.

＊

While seeing through the eyes of your role-model, feel your role-model's love for a person who you find difficult.

Experience the feelings and sensations. Describe this person from your role-model's (loving) point of view. Do your best to judge them favorably.

What does your role-model see in this person that generates love?

What is their potential?

＊

Absorb the love that you generated with this meditation, and feel how it increases and strengthens this person's positive qualities.

While this is already a high level, we can go even higher. Now, try to feel how God is watching over every part of the world. The truth is, He loves each and every person—including the person with whom you've had a hard time!

Imagine a big white light coming from God, and going through you. This light contains wonderful feelings of love, acceptance, and patience. Absorb these qualities and internalize them deeply. Now, project them from yourself to the person of your choosing, and imagine this person absorbing the light you have sent. Feel how the light connects both of you to God.

Put your two hands over your heart, right over left. Breath deeply, and let yourself enjoy the positive feelings of this unity.

Say aloud:

> *We are all created in the image of God. It is possible for me to love and to be loved and appreciated, and also [Insert the name of the person with whom you have had difficulties.] is deserving love. [find a quality that he/she is good in] I express gratitude, God, that You created both me and [insert name.] Each of us. Please help us, God, to learn to love and cherish all the goodness that you give. Teach us how to increase all that is positive within ourselves, and all of creation."*

To finish, bring your consciousness back to your senses and physical body. Move whenever you're ready. Open your eyes. Feel thankful for the time that you have devoted to connecting with God, however long it was.

With this meditation you have increased positivity within yourself, and weakened negativity—all without fighting. By increasing light, darkness disappears by itself.

Write in your journal. What have you experienced emotionally, physically, and mentally?

What fears have you overcome, and how did you do it? This simple writing process will change how you experience and respond to life's challenges.

Apply the inner lessons of this meditation, and you will increase the love that you feel for all people around you. This is a practice. A life-long practice of loving your fellow human beings; it's a fundamental attitude of one who is walking in the ways of God, practicing Kabbalistic meditation, and spiritual growth.

Chapter 3:
Meditations on Fear

In its simplest form, fear is how we defend ourselves against physical, emotional or spiritual harm.

Fears often originate from a significant traumatic experience that leaves a lasting impact. For example, someone who grew up in a financially disadvantaged home might carry a fear of poverty into their adult life.

Fear has its place. There is, for instance, the fear of making a poor decision. The due diligence you undertake on account of this fear is healthy.

However, if the fear stops you from doing anything postive and especialy things that are esential, it's an unhealthy, stultifying fear. Fear and stress, when experienced at unhealthy levels over time:

- debilitate your ability think clearly and concentrate,
- weaken the immune system,
- lead to feelings of depression and helplessness,
- cause high blood pressure, premature aging, hair loss, insomnia, headaches, bodily discomfort, and digestive issues.

It is essential to recognize the impact these emotions can have on our overall well-being, and take steps to manage and heal them.
What might not be obvious, however, is that our fear is really—the fear of *God*.

When we do something wrong, and believe that we are hiding from God...God hides from us. This is when we might experience "bad things", and fail to perceive that God is standing behind it all, waiting for us to return.

However, we attack the messenger and fail to listen to the message. We're like an angry dog that forgets the master who is striking it, and instead bites the master's stick. In the same way, when God is striking us, we cry out against the stick.

A far better thing to do is to listen to the message behind it. To elevate ourselves and look for the clues that God leaves for us to find.

When we do this, we will find ourselves surrounded by God's presence—precisely in the pain—where He will reveal ways in which we can self correct. However, we must learn to stand with God within the fear. We have to reach past the stick, to arrive at the knowledge of what is behind it.

When you are stuck by fear, there is a technique that you can turn to. In the language of the kabbalah, it is called:

Elevating the fear back to its Source.

We're going to ask God to show us how to elevate an unhealthy fear and to replace it with productive emotions, so that we can perform our role in the world in the best way possible—with joy and satisfaction. Authentic Kabbalistic meditations teach you to control your mind, and to release the grip of illusions and obstacles that keep you from connecting with God.

Meditation 11: Meditation to Heal Fear (1)

Nullify and replace negative images and feelings; create new pictures and emotions that are deep, vibrant, and fill you with love.

Before practicing this meditation, say the prayer:

Please God, with your compassion, help me to learn a new way to manage my fear and anxiety. Every time I feel fear and anxiety, I will ask You to speedily nullify and replace my negative feelings with a positive ones.

Think about something that causes you a negative fear, the kind that blocks or disturbs you. Use the power of your imagination to create an image of what this fear looks like.

Imagine how this fear would change if you had no doubt that its challenges are designed only to strengthen your connection with God. Meditate on how it will look and feel when you have the inner strength and ability to act how you most want in this situation.

Use the power of your imagination to create an image

of how your equanimity looks. Add more colors. Make the picture bigger, and incorporate any other images you might commonly have within your mind. Take notice of all your sences at this time. For example, add a positive voice, which represents the voice of God within you. This voice should encourage and reassure you that you can achieve your desired state.

✳

Think of the negative picture you imagined in your present state of fear and anxiety. Put your hand on your heart and say to God, silently or verbally:

> *Please God, nullify and replace this negative picture I have in my mind, with the desired image I've created.*

You can say it again and again. or even saying the same thing in different words while imagining the picture of your present state becoming darker, smaller and drifting away. Imagine the image of your desired state becoming lighter, more colorful, vivd and replacing everything else.

Repeat this process a few times. work on doing it more quickly every time, make sure that each time you finish, to thank God, and then open your eyes.

This positive practice can follow you into daily life. When you are experiencing fear, try putting your hand on your heart, close your eyes and say: **"Please God, nullify and replace."**

Then open your eyes while you are saying Thank You to God. If it was not enough, do the full process again and again.

Journal

Write what you experienced emotionally, physically and mentally. Have you overcome and nullified your fear? Or, have you been able to approach your feelings of fear in a new way? This is simple and powerful. It's a process that can change your experience of life's challenges, and heal unhealthy patterns of thought and emotion.

Meditation 12: Meditation to Heal Fear (2) Imagine a Positive Future

Envision a positive future, free from fear. Shift your focus from negative thoughts to hopeful possibilities. By connecting with these positive images and asking for divine support, you align your desires with a higher purpose and invite transformative change into your life.

Most fears are time bound. You imagine something bad happening, and you also imagine that there's nothing you can do about it. Nobody knows what the future holds, but psychologically, we're more likely to think negative thoughts than positive thoughts about the unknown.

Kabbalah teaches the exact opposite as it is written Even if a sharp sword is resting on one's thought he shouldn't hold back from (asking for) mercy." Also in our emotions we must remember that God works in mysterious ways and we can not phathom how God will save us.

However, just as you can imagine a bad thing, you can also imagine a good thing. It's not silly or delusional. Most of our thoughts about the future are illusory, and speculative at best.

The future is anyone's guess. Because it's completely up to God. We know that he is the ultimate good. Just as there are negative fears that stop you in your tracks, there are negative thoughts (which may be tied to fears) that you can have about the future, and these are not serving you.

Breathe. Think about your fear. Try to pinpoint when your fear will arise in the future.

Breathe again, and imagine yourself walking towards your future, in a positive way—without the fear. Create a picture of this positive future, which is waiting for you.

Feel the positive emotions that this future awakens within you. Pull yourself into the picture of your future, and pull the picture into you.

Ask God:

"Please God, bring this wonderful picture that I see inside of me to be reality in my life."
You can be more specific by describing in your inner-prayer why you feel this is the right thing that you need in your life.

Of course, we're not always sure. That's why it's appropriate to add: "...if this will be good for me."

You can even offer that when the positive thing you are praying for becomes reality —you will do a noble act, which may be challenging but must be something you can (and will) accomplish.

Meditation 13: Meditation to Heal Trauma

Use elevated consciousness to provide comfort and clarity to your inner child. By connecting with divine light and merging with God's presence, you can heal negative memories and gain strength, fostering a more positive future.
Many people suffer from the negative effects of traumatic experiences. Many things can cause trauma. Not just 'big things.' You can live a wonderful life and have trauma. We develop responses, both positive and negative; what we accept as a way of life might be how we have learned to respond to trauma.

Here is an effective kabbalistic meditation technique, which brings the light of God (which is beyond time) from the present—to heal our past—in order to enjoy a better future.

If you have never seen a surgery, viewing one without any explanation or even knowing that it is a life saving procedure, can be traumatic. Now, imagine viewing the same procedure with comforting explanations given to you by the surgeon.

While you might not feel comfortable, there would be less trauma that you would experience.

A guiding presence is a powerful thing.

Our goal in the following meditation is to connect to your past to give comfort and explanations for your inner child. The way you experience trauma is from your child's point of view—even if you are an adult.

This meditation is not meant to replace professional care. It is not a substitute for professional medical advice, diagnosis or treatment. This meditation should not be attempted without the guidance of a trained professional. please refer to the foot note above in Meditation 5a. If you're dealing with acute trauma, or intense emotional distress, do not do this mediation alone. Rather, seek the guidance of a trained professional who specializes in trauma therapy.

Begin with the Foundation.

Once you are in the meditative state, be aware of what emotion you are feeling at that moment. If it is negative, try to reconnect to God, with joy and happiness. Go higher and higher, with every breath, until you are surrounded with a comforting bliss. Allow the bright light of God to fill your heart. Transforming negative emotions into happiness deeply affects your soul, and the entire world. Allow the light of the Creator to flow into you. Kabbalah teaches that only by connecting to God is true happiness and love achieved.

Once you have reached the height of your meditative state, begin to contemplate God's oneness and merge with Him. Nullify yourself within Him. Know that He is All, and the source of all love and all good. Know that you are very much loved.

Imagine a line. One side represents the past, and the other side represents the future. The point where you stand is the present.

Feel your strength, which you have gained through the previous stages of this meditation. God is now filling you with consciousness.

Now, look back into your past and choose a **mildly** negative memory (not the traumatic one) when you were lacking consciousness, and unaware of God's presence.

Imagine that you—yourself at this moment— visits your past self in the negative memory. Envision yourself detached from your past self, as if you are a separate entity observing the scene. In this meditative state visualize bestowing your present self's inner strength and awareness upon your past self. Meditate on giving your past self comfort and clarity.

After you feel that your past self is more aware of God's presence, depart as you would from a dear friend. Open your eyes with a feeling of gratitude for the important lesson you have learned and that you were able to give to your past self.

The next time you practice this meditation, try going deeper into the past. However, wait to deal with the truly traumatic memories. *(see above footnote)*

Be patient with yourself. It takes time and practice to develop the spiritual, mental and emotional strength to perform these techniques in one sitting.
The harder the past experience, the more time and patience you'll need to bring light to your past.

You can pause the stream in your mind, and take time to explain to you as a child how much life is more than that difficult experience. The child needs to go through this, and even though it is extremely hard—things will start to get better. You will feel the light and presence of God once again.

Imagine how you as a child receives these comforts, and takes them deep into heart, changing your perspective.

In the same way that you comfort your own child who is screaming in the dentist's chair by holding his hand—all you can do is consciously hold your inner child's hand and explain with love that it is for his own good, so he knows that he is not alone.

This consciousness is a comfort.

Just like when you have an old friend, and you visit him to see how he needs help, you can go back to your past and visit who you used to be.

Give those different parts of yourself the comfort that comes from your present knowledge.

We are all children in front of God. We cannot comprehend his wisdom, greatness, endless love and compassion. Believe that God wants your ultimate good. Use that belief to develop more faith and trust when it's hard—this gives you the power to heal yourself and your inner child.

Separate from the experience.

Reclaim yourself.

Bring our whole being, from the past, present and future, to a new level of intimacy with God.

Chapter 4: Meditation for Anger

Relinquish and let go fo anger. This is a challenge, because anger is usually the worst emotion to show.

Imagine feeling so angry, you are ready to throw your family's expensive vase at someone. At that exact moment, a door opens.
Who is it?
> Your Father!
He gives you a severe look, that says don't you dare! Your anger is probably going to dissipate, because of his authority over you.

Not a good example? Think of a higher authority. Somebody in whose presence you could not stay angry. This is a person with enough power to return you to an awareness of your behavior, despite the anger.

Now, maybe you don't break the vase, but instead keep your angry speech.
But—what if you're in court, in front of a judge, who is just waiting for you to open your mouth and say one thing that's negative. So he can jail you.
You'll be forced to bite your tongue.
What if this judge has a machine that can read your mind? You'd be forced to control your thoughts!

This shows us the following: We lose control because we believe that we can act without facing any consequences.
Consequences for anger are severe.
The Jewish sages teach us that someone who is

overcome with anger brings into the world negative spiritual powers, which will control or even attack him.

If you break things out of anger, it is considered a denial of God. (It's best not to even look at the face of someone who is angry.)

According to the Kabbalah someone who becomes angry loses the spiritual gains he earned with his hard work—like a child who works for days to build a tower with building blocks, and in one moment of anger he breaks it down.

We should run from anger.
At the very least, learn to control it.
Gaining control over your anger is a battle that must be fought and won. Even if it takes many years.

According to the mystical master, Rabbi Chaim Vital, anger is a result of pride. To uproot the source of anger, it's important to work on humility.
This means letting go of your ego, acknowledging your limitations, embracing a modest and open mindset, recognizing your place in the world, and treating people with kindness and respect.

The process of overcoming anger is the way to becoming a better person. It is self-transcendence.

An essential virtue.

You can use meditation to reduce your feelings of anger. We'll explore two techniques. One to use actively during a conflict, and the other to release negative emotions you've stored. These techniques will help you manage and transform challenging emotional experiences.

Meditation 14: Anger Reducing Meditation

Increase your awareness to choose positivity over negativity. In your deep breathing, dissolve the barriers of anger, fostering a deeper connection with God and enhancing self-control.

By awakening your awareness, you will decrease the amount of time that you remain angry. Eventually, you will catch your anger the moment you feel it. Then you'll have a choice: to walk the path of anger, or the path of positivity.

Your goal is to awaken to your choice at the earliest possible moment. (Perhaps, even before you become angry!) This way you're still in a position of self-control, so you can prevent your anger from increasing.

Remove yourself. Physical separation is best, and if that's not possible, isolate yourself in your mind. Close your eyes. Hold your breath for a moment. Release it slowly. Focus on the experience of your breathing. Imagine you are breathing clean light in and out. With every exhale, you are expelling all your negative emotions, and making space for new light to enter.

Think about your relationship with God. How precious it is, and how important it is for you to improve. Choose to remove any barriers to your intimacy with Him.

*

Imagine how your anger and the negativity you feel form a wall between you and the Source of light. Try to increase your thirst and yearning to reconnect with Him, and feel more joy.

*

Ask Him to help you overcome your barrier. Tell Him the reason that you need to break the wall down is to connect with Him closely. (one can even imagine breaking down the wall or it melting)

*

As you speak these words of prayer, imagine they are beautiful birds that fly over the wall. More birds pass. The light increases and starts to dissolve the wall. You feel the warmth of the light of God surrounding you. Every breath brings more light of hope and love into your heart.

Express your gratitude. Ask God to allow you to awaken to your point of choice much sooner, and realize that every challenging situation is just an opportunity to practice this meditation and strengthen your connection to Hashem.

If you have a meditation diary, write your experience, and record the date. You will see your progress.

Chapter 5: Defining Your Purpose

- Who am I ?
- Why am I here?
- In this family?
- With this life?
- What should I do?
- Where did I come from?
- Where am I going?

When you can answer these questions, you will have joy, a feeling of purpose and completion.

In Hebrew, if you change your life according to these principles, you are called a chozer b'teshuva, literally translated to *one who returns with answers*, Repents and restores the original state.
We learn that all people are made in the image of God.
But how is this possible, when God has no form?
To understand this we can look at the words of King David, in Psalm 102:
"I am like a bird of the wilderness."
King David did not grow wings and a beak! Rather, in all of his trevails running from his enemies, he had something in common with a bird that wandered alone in the desert.

So too, when God created man in His image, it means that He gave man something in common with God.

What is it?

To find the answer, we must look deeply into the name of God: Elokim. The meaning of this name is that God has all powers, and these powers are completely different from the powers of a human being.

For example, when you build using wood, all you can do is reshape what has already grown in the forest. You cannot create from nothing the raw material of wood. You must take wood that was already created.

Once you've completed your creation, it stands independently. It doesn't rely on you for its existence. In contrast, Hashem created everything from nothing and continuously sustains life, ensuring His creations endure. Should God withdraw His sustaining force even for a moment, everything would cease to exist. This ongoing renewal is why Hebrew prayers mention that Hashem constantly renews the creation of the entire world each day.

Understanding this, we recognize why the name Elokim signifies the owner of all powers. Hashem not only created man but entrusted him with the governance of countless worlds, empowering him to lead them through his actions, speech, and thoughts. When man acts positively, he channels a positive flow into these worlds.

Conversely, if he acts negatively, heaven forbid, it obstructs the abundance and blocks the pathways through which each world receives its sustenance.

When a person performs a good deed, speaks kindly, or even thinks positively, he nourishes and revitalizes different powers and heavenly worlds. This enhances their light and holiness, as reflected in the verse from Yishayahu, "I will put my words in your mouth to plant the heavens and to establish the earth." The sages of the Torah teach that Torah scholars are considered builders of the world. They strengthen the upper worlds, drawing down the light of Hashem and bringing a flow of abundance to our world.

Conversely, if someone, heaven forbid, acts, speaks, or thinks negatively, he diminishes the light and holiness of the heavenly worlds, leading to darkness and obscuring the light of Hashem.

This understanding sheds light on the verse stating that Hashem created man in His image. Just as Hashem is the master and sustainer of all powers in all worlds, orchestrating and guiding them every moment according to His will, He also endowed mankind with the ability to open and close countless powers and worlds. This is explained thoroughly in the deep books of Kabbalah, where the effectiveness of each individual is according to the level of his soul.

The Kabbalist Rabbi Moshe Chaim Luzzatto, in his book Derech Hashem, explains that all of creation, with its different dimensions, was crafted according to divine wisdom for the ultimate purpose of the entire creation. Each aspect of creation is designed with its final purpose in mind.

Therefore, God not only created these diverse parts but also maintains their existence, giving them the opportunity to fulfill their role in bringing about the final purpose of creation.

God's involvement in creation is not passive; He actively ensures that every detail and every individual contributes to the fulfillment of the creation's final purpose. If you wonder whether this makes us mere puppets, the Sages teach that free will is a fundamental quality in the creation of man. (This topic is extensive and would be better suited for a separate, dedicated work.)

The initial stages of creation were entirely spiritual, with the physical aspects emerging much later. Therefore, we learn that any physical existence has a spiritual root that existed long before the physical creation. This design was intentional, with each part of creation fulfilling its purpose in the final total rectification.
As long as a part of creation continues to serve its purpose, it will continue to exist. The master of the universe observes the actions, speech, thoughts, and desires of each individual.

Through this connection, you receive spiritual, emotional, and physical sustenance to fulfill your purpose.

Do We Have a Choice?
The creation of humankind differs from all other parts

of creation—whether physical, like plants, animals, and minerals, or spiritual, like angels and heavenly creatures. The unique quality of humankind is the free will and ability Hashem granted us to achieve completion (shlemut) or its opposite. Mankind is created to be an active participant in Hashem's creation, not merely a passive observer.

According to this principle, Hashem's observation of mankind differs from His observation of the rest of creation.

For the rest of creation, Hashem's observation dictates their actions, making it impossible for them to deviate from their function. His observation not only guides but also sustains them. Instead of dictating each individual's actions, Hashem leads them like a person guiding a donkey, directing them in the right direction. Mankind, however, is seen as if Hashem is following their lead. The way Hashem follows mankind's actions is by rewarding and punishing—rewards and punishments are direct consequences of human actions, speech, thoughts, and intentions, much like a coachman holding the reins behind the horse.

Meditation 15: Trust In God's Guidance

Reflect on the divine presence. Align with Hashem's light, which dispels negativity and reinforces the understanding that everything unfolds according to His will, including your path.

Start with the Foundation Meditation; take two minutes or more to isolate yourself from the world. Turn off everything. Do not let anything bother you. Avoid unnecessary distractions.
Sit with your back erect and your head straight. When the spine is in its natural, upright position, it is easier to connect. Smile a bit; do not be too serious.

Take a breath and hold it for a moment. Then, let it out slowly. Focus on the sounds and sensations of your breathing. Close your eyes and bring your breath to the center of your mind. Imagine yourself breathing in clean light and exhaling light. With every exhale, relax even more.

While breathing, reflect on life and how its events unfold, seeking to recognize Hashem's hand at work. Identify instances where you have directly observed the Hand of Hashem altering reality. Acknowledge that everything comes from Hashem—no power or person in the world can do good or harm except through Him! Hashem is supreme, the ultimate source of everything, and all that He does is purely good. He constantly renews creation, every day. The God who made Heaven and Earth is here with you.

As you meditate on these truths, feel Hashem's light surrounding you. As you breathe, sense the light entering your body, healing you, and dispelling negative thoughts and emotions. Ask Hashem to fill you with pure, truthful thoughts as you inhale. Since the goal of any practice is to condition behavior through repetition, the practice of perceiving the world as an expression of divine Oneness can begin as soon as you gain consciousness.

Where is Hashem leading you? What does He want from you?

Each time a negative thought enters your mind, greet it, remind yourself that Hashem is in control and knows what He is doing, and that all He does is purely good. Then, return to your meditation as the thought drifts away and disappears.

When you have finished, bring your consciousness back to your senses and physical body. Gradually introduce movement, and when you are ready, open your eyes. Be thankful for the time you have devoted to connecting with Hashem, even if only for a moment. As you repeat this meditation and increase the light and love within yourself, you will find that negativity diminishes without struggle, just as darkness disappears when light is increased.

Journal your experiences—emotionally, physically, and mentally. What new tools have you learned, and how can you apply them to better your life? Try to write down at least one tool that you can use daily to stay focused on God consciousness (knowing that Hashem is here and in charge). This practice is simple yet powerful. Keeping God consciousness in your mind can transform how you navigate life's obstacles.

This subject can be explored further and expanded into a large book. With Hashem's help, we will do more on this topic, bli neder (without making a binding vow).

"I call on heaven and earth to witness that any individual, man or woman, Jew or Gentile, freeman or slave, can have Ruach HaKodesh (Divine Inspiration) descend upon him."

*

What are the 7 Laws given to mankind?

It is impossible to explain the fullness of the sheva mitzvot here. What is offered is only a glimpse. In fact, each mitzvot is a full category in and of itself. Collectively, the 7 comandments are a very large portion of Halachah (the Jewish Code of Law).

The sheva mitzvot are the basic requirements of human morality.

The sheva mitzvot connect Adam (mankind) with God and enables those who guard them out of love of God to enter Olam Haba (Eternal life/heaven).

They encompass a legal system, a spiritual framework, and principles of morals and ethics collectively.

The 7 mitzvot are the pathway to a more meaningful life.
They are the future system by which all the nations will live by as prophesied.

1. Do not commit idolatry

This mitzvah is the most important of them all because humans have the freewill to do their own will or do God's will. Whenever one serves or prays to anything other than the one true God, this is idolatry.

2. Do not commit sexual sins

As recorded in Bereishit 2:24, "That is why a man leaves his father and mother, and cleaves to his wife".

The Sages extrapolate from here that homosexuality, incest, adultery, rape, beastiality etc., are all prohibited.

The sexual desire is very powerful and when it is used incorrectly it can cause terrible damage to oneself and your spouse and creation as a whole, Hashem forbid.

However, if one practices sexual desire in a proper context, it can elevate all of creation!

3. Do not commit bloodshed

Killing to proctect from being killed, is permitted. Aside from this, all bloodshed is prohibited. This includes abortion, suicide, aiding suicide and/or indirect murder.

4. Do not commit theft/steal

Although this, in fact all these holy commandments, seem to be simple and obvious, theft can happen in the most subtle of ways. For example, misusing time at work is a subtle form of theft.

5. Do not commit injustice

To set up an objective legal system to uphold laws. Many legal systems, nobles, wealthy people, intelligent people, mighty people etc. have taken advantage of the less fortunate and weak. The Torah states that Hashem wants the fortunate to give tzeddakah (charity). The poor exist so they can pray to Hashem for help and for the fortunate to take pity on the less fortunate and give tzeddakah (charity). The opposite of this is injustice.

6. Do not commit blasphemy

Once a person takes upon these holy, precious laws, his/her public and private comportment must bring honor to God. If one does the opposite is committing blasphemy. Moreover, if one allows the difficulties of life to blind him/her that everything happens for good and thus speaks negatively, God forbid, of the Creator, commits a grievous sin.

7. Do not eat a limb from a living animal

In ancient times and even in present day, some people eat a portion of an animal while it is still living. This is cruelty. Also, "flesh with its life, which is its blood you shall not eat" (Bereishit 9:4). Actually, causing unnecessary pain to any creature is cruelty. In deed, this final mitzvah can be summarized in the following way - be merciful to all creation.

**

Describe your experience with your mediation				
Date				
Mentaly				
Emotionaly				
Physicaly				
Did letters apear?				
Was there a change from the last time?				

Who we are and what we do

"Yeshivas Hamekubalim Nefesh Hachaim" merits being located in Yerushalayim on Har Tzion adjacent to Kever David Hamelech. The yeshiva is a pioneer in publishing siddurim and machzorim with the Kavanot of the Ariza"l specially geared to the beginner. Our siddurim are printed in an unabridged, clear format. They include instructions, introductions, and various customs written in a clear and easy style specified for our day and age. They also feature various prayers, intentions, charts and expanded Roshei Teivos to assist those wishing to enter these gates of wisdom. All this is done with nice fonts and typesettings which facilitate easy reading. Many of those who got used to our siddurim claim they cannot substitute it for any other kind.

Throughout the years we've expanded the repertoire of seforim we publish to incorporate a few types of siddurim, machzorim, tikun chatzot and books on various subjects. We also plan on publishing B'ezrat Hashem, a Tehilim, seforim on halachot and customs, commentaries on the Ariza"l writing and other Kabbalah seforim, Siddurim for women, Seder for Hoshana Raba night, shavuos night, Shvi'i Shel Pesach, books on segulos and personal prayers, a book of songs for Shabbos and festivals, Seder for Chanukas Habayit, Seder for a Brit Yitzchak, and prayers for the illui nashama of the niftarim.
 "Yeshivas Hamekubalim Nefesh Hachaim" merits encouragement from gedolei Torah of our generation

and is especially endorsed by Rabbi Yitzchak Goldstein Shlit"a Rosh Yeshiva of Diaspora Yeshiva.

We are presently occupied with publishing our siddur -"Siddur Chen" with english introductions explinations and instructions. Many years of painstaking work was put into it so far. It is a result of much effort of our group that gathers to study the introductions and Kavanot of the Ariza"l. The siddur incorporates introductions, charts and explanations to ease the understanding of these Kavanot. We are simultaneously working on Ashkenaz, Sefard, and Safardi siddurim, in three languages, Hebrew, English and Spanish.

Is it permitted to translate and why?

Many ask if is it permitted to translate Kabbalah literature into other languages. There are multiple answers to this question. The main response is that the unfortunate situation today is that there are some charlatans out there, many of whom aren't even Jewish, that present themselves as Mekubalim. Unfortunately , many Jews fall prey to them. Therefore anyone with the power to protest has the obligation to do so. He should also publicize as much as possible the correct way to approach these gates of wisdom. He should educate the masses that there is no way to fulfill their desire of attaining this wisdom other than the authentic Jewish way that was passed down for generations. If anyone tries to attain this wisdom elsewhere he will destroy rather than rectify. Therefore, we feel it to be not only permitted but important to translate these seforim of Kabbalah to make our people aware of the aforementioned.

Another reason to translate these seforim is that many observant people throughout the world feel distant from spirituality. All their Torah and prayer are done by rote and just to fulfill their basic obligation to feel free to be able to move onto matters they find more interesting. We are confident that if they would taste the sweetness of the wisdom of Kabbalah, or even just some insights into what they are already doing, they would quickly be transformed to serious Ovdei Hashem. As they begin to see and understand how the whole Torah is connected to, and effects the higher worlds, they will get a new realization of what Torah is, and a renewed spirit.

Sharing the merit with you

It goes without saying that these projects are costly. Production is not progressing as quickly as it should fitting such a worthy project. We therefore extend our offer to all of Am Yisroel to participate in this tremendously holy project. Please take a generous part in funding the continuation of these important works. These are works of rishonim who are compared to angels. Through helping produce these works one can arouse the zchusim of the Rabbis who brought this profound wisdom down to us. This will also be the cause of elevation to their souls, and in this merit they will pray for us all to receive limitless bounty and blessing, Amen.

What else is in it for you

The Chofetz Chaim wrote in his sefer Ahavas Chesed that there are people who want to do something special in memory of a loved one. Sometimes they make a nice expensive tombstone with golden letters and nice flowers.

Some add nice plants and the like and spend a fortune on these items. They think this will cause some pleasure to their departed relative. They are gravely mistaken. If heaven forbid a relative passes on and didn't leave any progeny behind, instead of investing in the above items, they should make an everlasting memory for them with a mitzvah that will endure for generations. If he doesn't have the means for this he should at least donate a Sefer in his memory, for the public to learn from, and write the name of the departed inside. This way whenever someone learns from it it will cause pleasure to the nifter. The Chofetz Chaim concludes that he's seen many do this.

This merit is multiplied many times over if one would dedicate the publishing of a new Siddur like the one we are working on. This would help many Yidden throughout the world pray to God with the proper kavana and to draw down to the world a spiritual and physical flow of blessings in all areas. This would also bring the geula closer. How meritorious would these sponsors be in this world and the next! They will be among the mezakei harabim that regarding them is written "They are like the stars forever", for this is a merit that lasts forever.

לזכרון עולם

יוחנן יעקב אדוורד פרינג ז״ל

גר תושב

JOHN JACK EDWARD PRING Z"L

A GER TOSHAV

5781 / 2021 - 5699 / 1939

DEDICATED BY
DIXIE CHAYA PRING

לזכרון עולם

Dedicated in memory of
A beloved mother and a father I never knew

Diane Hope bat Adam
Victor Jr ben Victor Sr

May it be a merit for thier generations
May their soul be bound in the bond of eternal life

Dedicated in the memory of
Hadasah Rachel bat Moshe and Chana
תנצב״ה

Dedicated in the memory of

לאינה בת אנה

יוסף בן חנה

רבקה בת בתיה

נח בן דב

לאה בת רחל

תנצב"ה

Dedicated in the memory of

דבורה בת שרה

טפחה בת טפחה

מזל בת דינה

אדל בת אשר

תנצב"ה

Have your dedication in one of our publications So it be a lasting merit for you and your loved one. Please conntact us at KingDavidKabbalah.com